CW01151937

Vegan Air Fryer Cookbook

*Cook and Taste 50+ High-Protein Recipes.
Kickstart Muscles and Body Transformation,
Kill Hunger and Feel More Energetic*

By

Sabrina Malcontenta

© **Copyright 2021 by (Sabrina Malcontenta - All rights reserved.**

This document is geared towards providing exact and reliable information in regards to the topic and issue covered. The publication is sold with the idea that the publisher is not required to render accounting, officially permitted, or otherwise, qualified services. If advice is necessary, legal or professional, a practiced individual in the profession should be ordered.

- From a Declaration of Principles which was accepted and approved equally by a Committee of the American Bar Association and a Committee of Publishers and Associations.

In no way is it legal to reproduce, duplicate, or transmit any part of this document in either electronic means or in printed format. Recording of this publication is strictly prohibited and any storage of this document is not allowed unless with written permission from the publisher. All rights reserved.

The information provided herein is stated to be truthful and consistent, in that any liability, in terms of inattention or otherwise, by any usage or abuse of any policies, processes, or directions contained within is the solitary and utter responsibility of the recipient reader. Under no circumstances will any legal responsibility or blame be held against the publisher for any reparation, damages, or monetary loss due to the information herein, either directly or indirectly.

Respective authors own all copyrights not held by the publisher.

The information herein is offered for informational purposes solely, and is universal as so. The presentation of the information is without contract or any type of guarantee assurance.

The trademarks that are used are without any consent, and the publication of the trademark is without permission or backing by the trademark owner. All trademarks and brands within this book are for clarifying purposes only and are the owned by the owners themselves, not affiliated with this document.

Contents

Introduction 7
   What is Cooking Vegan? 9
   What advantages would veganism have? 10
   Air Fryer 12
   Air fryer's Working Process: 14
   Tips for using an Air Fryer 16
   Outcome 19

CHAPTER 1: Breakfast Recipes 20
   1. *Toasted French toast* 20
   2. *Vegan Casserole* 22
   3. *Vegan Omelet* 24
   4. *Waffles with Vegan chicken* 27
   5. *Tempeh Bacon* 30
   6. *Delicious Potato Pancakes* 33

CHAPTER 2: Air Fryer Main Dishes 35
   1. **Mushroom 'n Bell Pepper Pizza** 36
   2. *Veggies Stuffed Eggplants* 38
   3. *Air-fried Falafel* 40
   4. *Almond Flour Battered Wings* 42
   5. *Spicy Tofu* 43
   6. *Sautéed Bacon with Spinach* 44
   7. *Garden Fresh Veggie Medley* 45
   8. *Colorful Vegetable Croquettes* 46
   9. *Cheesy Mushrooms* 48
   10. *Greek-style Roasted Vegetables* 49

11.	Vegetable Kabobs with Simple Peanut Sauce	51
12.	Hungarian Mushroom Pilaf	52
13.	Chinese cabbage Bake	54
14.	Brussels sprouts With Balsamic Oil	56
15.	Aromatic Baked Potatoes with Chives	56
16.	Easy Vegan "chicken"	57
17.	Paprika Vegetable Kebab's	59
18.	Spiced Soy Curls	60
19.	Cauliflower & Egg Rice Casserole	62
20.	Hollandaise Topped Grilled Asparagus	63
21.	Crispy Asparagus Dipped In Paprika-garlic Spice	64
22.	Eggplant Gratin with Mozzarella Crust	65
23.	Asian-style Cauliflower	67
24.	**Two-cheese Vegetable Frittata**	**68**
25.	Rice & Beans Stuffed Bell Peppers	70
26.	Parsley-loaded Mushrooms	71
27.	Cheesy Vegetable Quesadilla	72
28.	Creamy 'n Cheese Broccoli Bake	73
29.	Sweet & Spicy Parsnips	75
30.	Zucchini with Mediterranean Dill Sauce	76
31.	Zesty Broccoli	78
32.	Chewy Glazed Parsnips	79
33.	Hoisin-glazed Bok Choy	80
34.	Green Beans with Okra	81
35.	Celeriac with some Greek Yogurt Dip	82
36.	Wine & Garlic Flavored Vegetables	83
37.	Spicy Braised Vegetables	84

CHAPTER 3: Air Fryer Snack Side Dishes and Appetizer Recipes......... 87

1.	Crispy 'n Tasty Spring Rolls	88
2.	Spinach & Feta Crescent Triangles	89
3.	Healthy Avocado Fries	90
4.	Twice-fried Cauliflower Tater Tots	91
5.	Cheesy Mushroom & Cauliflower Balls	92
6.	Italian Seasoned Easy Pasta Chips	94
7.	Thai Sweet Potato Balls	95
8.	Barbecue Roasted Almonds	96
9.	Croissant Rolls	97
10.	Curry' n Coriander Spiced Bread Rolls	98
11.	Scrumptiously Healthy Chips	100
12.	Kid-friendly Vegetable Fritters	101
13.	Avocado Fries	103
14.	Crispy Wings with Lemony Old Bay Spice	105
15.	Cold Salad with Veggies and Pasta	106
16.	Zucchini and Minty Eggplant Bites	108
17.	Stuffed Potatoes	109
18.	Paneer Cutlet	110
19.	Spicy Roasted Cashew Nuts	111

CHAPTER 4: Deserts 113

1.	Almond-apple Treat	113
2.	Pepper-pineapple With Butter-sugar Glaze	113
3.	True Churros with Yummy Hot Chocolate	114

Conclusion 117

Introduction

To have a good, satisfying life, a balanced diet is important. Tiredness and susceptibility to illnesses, many severe, arise from a lifestyle so full of junk food. Our community, sadly, does not neglect unsafe choices. People turn to immoral practices in order to satisfy desire, leading to animal torture. Two of the key explanations that people adhere to vegetarianism, a vegan-based diet that often excludes animal foods such as cheese, beef, jelly, and honey, are fitness and animal welfare.

It's essential for vegetarians to get the most nutrients out of any food, and that's where frying using an air fryer shines. The air fryer cooking will maintain as many nutrients as possible from beans and veggies, and the gadget makes it incredibly simple to cook nutritious food.

Although there are prepared vegan alternatives, the healthier choice, and far less pricey, is still to prepare your own recipes. This book provides the very first moves to being a vegan and offers 50 quick breakfast recipes, sides, snacks, and much more, so you have a solid base on which to develop.

This book will teach you all you need to thrive, whether you are either a vegan and only need more meal choices or have just begun contemplating transforming your diet.

What is Cooking Vegan?

In recent decades, vegetarianism has become quite common, as individuals understand just how toxic the eating patterns of civilization have become. We are a society that enjoys meat, and, unfortunately, we go to dishonest measures to get the food we like. More citizens are choosing to give up beef and, unlike vegans, other livestock items due to various health issues, ethical issues, or both. Their diet moves to one focused on plants, whole grains, beans, fruit, seeds, nuts, and vegan varieties of the common dish.

What advantages would veganism have?

There are a lot of advantages to a diet away from all animal items. Only a few includes:

- Healthier hair, skin, and nails
- High energy
- Fewer chances of flu and cold
- Fewer migraines

- Increased tolerance to cancer

- Strengthened fitness of the heart

Although research has proven that veganism will contribute to reducing BMI, it must not be followed for the mere sake of weight reduction. "Vegan" does not indicate "lower-calorie," and if you wish to reduce weight, other healthier activities, including exercising and consuming water, can complement the diet.

Air Fryer

A common kitchen gadget used to create fried foods such as beef, baked goods and potato chips is an air fryer. It provides a crunchy, crisp coating by blowing hot air across the food. This also leads to a chemical reaction commonly known as the Maillard effect, which happens in the presence of heat in between reducing sugar and amino acid. This adds to shifts in food color and taste. Due to the reduced amount of calories and fat, air-fried items are marketed as a healthier substitute to deep-fried foods.

Rather than fully soaking the food in fat, air-frying utilizes just a teaspoon to create a flavor and feel equivalent to deep-fried foods.

The flavor and appearance of the fried food in the air are similar to the deep fryer outcomes: On the surface, crispy; from the inside, soft. You do need to use a limited amount of oil, though, or any at all (based on what you're baking). But indeed, contrary to deep frying, if you agree to use only 1-2 teaspoons of plant-based oil with spices and you stuck to air-frying vegetables rather than anything else, air frying is certainly a better option.

The secret to weight loss, decreased likelihood of cardiovascular illness and better long-term wellbeing as we mature is any gadget that assists you and your friends in your vegetarian game.

Air fryer's Working Process:

The air fryer is a worktop kitchen gadget that operates in the same manner as a traditional oven. To become acquainted with the operating theory of the traditional oven, you will need a little study. The air fryer uses rotating hot air to fry and crisp your meal, close to the convection oven. In a traditional convection oven, the airflow relies on revolving fans, which blast hot air around to produce an even or equalized temperature dispersal throughout the oven.

This is compared to the upward airflow of standard ovens, where the warm place is typically the oven's tip. And although the air fryer is not quite like the convection oven, it is a great approximation of it in the field of airflow for most components. The gadget has an air inlet at the top that lets air in and a hot air outlet at the side. All of these features are used to monitor the temperature within the air fryer. Temperatures will rise to 230 ° C, based on the sort of air fryer you're buying.

In conjunction with any grease, this hot air is used for cooking the food in the bowl within the device, if you like. Yes, if you want a taste of the oil, you should apply more oil. To jazz up the taste of the meal, simply add a little more to the blend. But the key concept behind the air fryer is to reduce the consumption of calories and fat without reducing the amount of taste.

Using air frying rather than deep frying saves between 70-80 calories, according to researchers. The growing success of recipes for air fryers is simply attributed to its impressive performance. It is simple to use and less time-consuming than conventional ovens.

This is more or less a lottery win for people searching for healthy alternative to deep-frying, as demonstrated by its widespread popularity in many homes today. In contrast to conventional ovens or deep frying, the air fryer creates crispy, crunchy, wonderful, and far fewer fatty foods in less duration. For certain individuals like us; this is what distinguishes air fryer recipes.

Tips for using an Air Fryer

1. The food is cooked easily. Air fried, unlike conventional cooking techniques, cut the cooking time a great deal. Therefore, to stop burning the food or getting a not-so-great

flavor, it is best to hold a close eye on the gadget. Notice, remember that the smaller the food on the basket, the shorter the cooking period, which implies that the food cooks quicker.

2. You may need to reduce the temperature at first. Bear in mind that air fryers depend on the flow of hot air, which heats up rapidly. This ensures that it's better, to begin with, a low temperature so that the food cooks equally. It is likely that when the inside is already cooking, the exterior of the food is all cooked and begins to become dark or too dry.

3. When air fryers are in operation, they create some noise. If you are new to recipes for air fryers, you may have to realize that air fryers create noise while working. When it's in service, a whirring tone emanates from the device. However, the slight annoyance pales in contrast to the various advantages of having an air fryer.

4. Hold the grate within the container at all hours. As previously mentioned, the air fryer has a container inside it, where the food is put and permitted to cook. This helps hot air to flow freely around the food, allowing for even cooking.

5. Don't stuff the air fryer with so much food at once. If you plan to make a meal for one guy, with only one batch, you would most definitely be able to get your cooking right. If you're cooking for two or more individuals, you can need to

plan the food in groups. With a 4 - 5 quart air fryer, you can always need to cook in groups, depending on the size and sort of air fryer you have. This not only means that your device works longer but also keeps your food from cooking unevenly. You shouldn't have to turn the air fryer off as you pull out the basket since it simply turns off on its own until the basket is out. Often, make sure the drawer is completely retracted; otherwise, the fryer would not turn back on.

6. Take the basket out of the mix and mix the ingredients. You might need to move the food around or switch it over once every few minutes, based on the dish you're preparing and the time it takes to prepare your dinner.

The explanation for this is that even cooking can be done. Certain recipes involve the foods in the basket to shake and shuffle throughout the cooking phase. And an easy-to-understand checklist is given for each recipe to direct you thru the cycle.

7. The air fryer does not need cooking mist. It isn't needed. In order to prevent the urge to use non-stick frying spray in the container, you must deliberately take care of this. The basket is now coated with a non-stick covering, so what you need to do is fill your meal inside the container and push it back in.

Outcome

You can create nutritious meals very simply and fast, right in the comfort of your house. There are many excellent recipes for producing healthier meals and nutritious foods, which you can notice in the air fryer recipes illustrated in this book. However, you'll need to pay careful attention to the ingredients and know-how to easily use the air fryer to do this. To get straightforward guidance on installation and usage, you can need to refer to the company's manual.

CHAPTER 1: Breakfast Recipes

1. Toasted French toast

Preparation time: 2 minutes

Cooking time: 5 minutes

Servings: 1 people

Ingredients:

- ½ Cup of Unsweetened Shredded Coconut
- 1 Tsp. Baking Powder

- ½ Cup Lite Culinary Coconut Milk
- 2 Slices of Gluten-Free Bread (use your favorite)

Directions:

1. Stir together the baking powder and coconut milk in a large rimmed pot.
2. On a tray, layout your ground coconut.
3. Pick each loaf of your bread and dip it in your coconut milk for the very first time, and then pass it to the ground coconut, let it sit for a few minutes, then cover the slice entirely with the coconut.
4. Place the covered bread loaves in your air fryer, cover it, adjust the temperature to about 350 ° F and set the clock for around 4 minutes.
5. Take out from your air fryer until done, and finish with some maple syrup of your choice. French toast is done. Enjoy!

2. Vegan Casserole

Preparation time: 10-12 minutes

Cooking time: 15-20 minutes

Servings: 2-3 people

Ingredients:

- 1/2 cup of cooked quinoa
- 1 tbsp. of lemon juice
- 2 tbsp. of water
- 2 tbsp. of plain soy yogurt
- 2 tbsp. of nutritional yeast

- 7 ounces of extra-firm tofu about half a block, drained but not pressed
- 1/2 tsp. of ground cumin
- 1/2 tsp. of red pepper flakes
- 1/2 tsp. of freeze-dried dill
- 1/2 tsp. of black pepper
- 1/2 tsp. of salt
- 1 tsp. of dried oregano
- 1/2 cup of diced shiitake mushrooms
- 1/2 cup of diced bell pepper I used a combination of red and green
- 2 small celery stalks chopped
- 1 large carrot chopped
- 1 tsp. of minced garlic
- 1 small onion diced
- 1 tsp. of olive oil

Directions:

1. Warm the olive oil over medium-low heat in a big skillet. Add your onion and garlic and simmer till the onion is transparent (for about 3 to 6 minutes). Add

your bell pepper, carrot, and celery and simmer for another 3 minutes. Mix the oregano, mushrooms, pepper, salt, cumin, dill, and red pepper powder. Mix completely and lower the heat to low. If the vegetables tend to cling, stir regularly and add in about a teaspoon of water.

2. Pulse the nutritional yeast, tofu, water, yogurt, and some lemon juice in a food mixer until fluffy. To your skillet, add your tofu mixture. Add in half a cup of cooked quinoa. Mix thoroughly.

3. Move to a microwave-proof plate or tray that works for your air fryer basket.

4. Cook for around 15 minutes at about 350°F (or 18 to 20 minutes at about 330°F, till it turns golden brown).

5. Please take out your plate or tray from your air fryer and let it rest for at least five minutes before eating.

3. Vegan Omelet

Preparation time: 15 minutes

Cooking time: 16 minutes

Servings: 3 people

Ingredients:

- ½ cup of grated vegan cheese
- 1 tbsp. of water
- 1 tbsp. of brags
- 3 tbsp. of nutritional yeast
- ¼ tsp. of basil
- ¼ tsp. of garlic powder
- ¼ tsp. of onion powder
- ¼ tsp. of pepper
- ½ tsp. of cumin
- ½ tsp. of turmeric
- ¼ tsp. of salt
- ¼ cup of chickpea flour (or you may use any bean flour)
- ½ cup of finely diced veggies (like chard, kale, dried mushrooms, spinach, watermelon radish etc.)
- half a piece of tofu (organic high in protein kind)

Directions:

4. Blend all your ingredients in a food blender or mixer, excluding the vegetables and cheese.

5. Move the batter from the blender to a container and combine the vegetables and cheese in it. Since it's faster, you could use both hands to combine it.

6. Brush the base of your air fryer bucket with some oil.

7. Put a couple of parchment papers on your counter. On the top of your parchment paper, place a cookie cutter of your desire.

8. In your cookie cutter, push 1/6 of the paste. Then raise and put the cookie cutter on a different section of your parchment paper.

9. Redo the process till you have about 6 pieces using the remainder of the paste.

10. Put 2 or 3 of your omelets at the base of your air fryer container. Using some oil, brush the topsides of the omelets.

11. Cook for around 5 minutes at about 370 °, turn and bake for another 4 minutes or more if needed. And redo with the omelets that remain.

12. Offer with sriracha mayo or whatever kind of dipping sauce you prefer. Or use them for a sandwich at breakfast.

4. Waffles with Vegan chicken

Preparation time: 10 minutes

Cooking time: 15 minutes

Servings: 2 people

Ingredients:

Fried Vegan Chicken:

- ¼ to ½ teaspoon of Black Pepper
- ½ teaspoon of Paprika

- ½ teaspoon of Onion Powder
- ½ teaspoon of Garlic Powder
- 2 teaspoon of Dried Parsley
- 2 Cups of Gluten-Free Panko
- ¼ Cup of Cornstarch
- 1 Cup of Unsweetened Non-Dairy Milk
- 1 Small Head of Cauliflower

Yummy Cornmeal Waffles:

- ½ teaspoon of Pure Vanilla Extract
- ¼ Cup of Unsweetened Applesauce
- ½ Cup of Unsweetened Non-Dairy Milk
- 1 to 2 TB Erythritol (or preferred sweetener)
- 1 teaspoon Baking Powder
- ¼ Cup of Stoneground Cornmeal
- ⅔ Cup of Gluten-Free All-Purpose Flour

Toppings:

- Vegan Butter
- Hot Sauce
- Pure Maple Syrup

Directions:

For making your Vegan Fried Chicken:

1. Dice the cauliflower (you wouldn't have to be careful in this) into big florets and put it aside.

2. Mix the cornstarch and milk in a tiny pot.

3. Throw the herbs, panko, and spices together in a big bowl or dish.

4. In the thick milk mixture, soak your cauliflower florets, then cover the soaked bits in the prepared panko mix before putting the wrapped floret into your air fryer bucket.

5. For the remaining of your cauliflower, redo the same process.

6. Set your air fryer clock for around 15 minutes to about 400 ° F and let the cauliflower air fry.

For making you're Waffles:

1. Oil a regular waffle iron and warm it up.

2. Mix all your dry ingredients in a pot, and then blend in your wet ingredients until you have a thick mixture.

3. To create a big waffle, utilize ½ of the mixture and redo the process to create another waffle for a maximum of two persons.

To Organize:

1. Put on dishes your waffles, place each with ½ of the cooked cauliflower, now drizzle with the hot sauce, syrup, and any extra toppings that you want. Serve warm!

5. Tempeh Bacon

Preparation time: 15 minutes plus 2 hour marinating time

Cooking time: 10 minutes

Servings: 4 people

Ingredients:

- ½ teaspoon of freshly grated black pepper
- ½ teaspoon of onion powder
- ½ teaspoon of garlic powder
- 1 ½ teaspoon of smoked paprika
- 1 teaspoon of apple cider vinegar
- 1 tablespoon of olive oil (plus some more for oiling your air fryer)
- 3 tablespoon of pure maple syrup
- ¼ cup of gluten-free, reduced-sodium tamari
- 8 oz. of gluten-free tempeh

Directions:

1. Break your Tempeh cube into two parts and boil for about 10 minutes, some more if required. To the rice cooker bowl, add a cup of warm water. Then, put the pieces of tempeh into the steamer basket of the unit. Close the cover, push the button for heat or steam cooking (based on your rice cooker's type or brand), and adjust the steaming timer for around 10 minutes.

2. Let the tempeh cool completely before taking it out of the rice cooker or your steamer basket for around 5 minutes.

3. Now make the sauce while cooking the tempeh. In a 9" x 13" baking tray, incorporate all the rest of your ingredients and mix them using a fork. Then set it aside and ready the tempeh.

4. Put the tempeh steamed before and cooled on a chopping board, and slice into strips around 1/4' wide. Put each slice gently in the sauce. Then roll over each slice gently. Seal and put in the fridge for two to three hours or even overnight, rotating once or twice during the time.

5. Turn the bits gently one more time until you are about to create the tempeh bacon. And if you would like, you may spoon over any leftover sauce.

6. Put your crisper plate/tray into the air fryer if yours came with one instead of a built-in one. Oil the base of your crisper tray or your air fryer basket slightly with some olive oil or using an olive oil spray that is anti-aerosol.

7. Put the tempeh slices in a thin layer gently in your air fryer bucket. If you have a tiny air fryer, you will have

to air fry it in two or multiple rounds. Air fry for around 10-15 minutes at about 325 ° F before the slices are lightly golden but not burnt. You may detach your air fryer container to inspect it and make sure it's not burnt. It normally takes about 10 minutes.

6. Delicious Potato Pancakes

Preparation time: 5 minutes

Cooking time: 15 minutes

Servings: 4 people

Ingredients:

- black pepper according to taste
- 3 tablespoon of flour
- ¼ teaspoon of pepper
- ¼ teaspoon of salt
- ½ teaspoon of garlic powder
- 2 tablespoon of unsalted butter
- ¼ cup of milk
- 1 beaten egg
- 1 medium onion, chopped

Directions:

1. Preheat the fryer to about 390° F and combine the potatoes, garlic powder, eggs, milk, onion, pepper, butter, and salt in a small bowl; add in the flour and make a batter.

2. Shape around 1/4 cup of your batter into a cake.

3. In the fryer's cooking basket, put the cakes and cook for a couple of minutes.

4. Serve and enjoy your treat!

CHAPTER 2: Air Fryer Main Dishes

1. Mushroom 'n Bell Pepper Pizza

Preparation time: 5 minutes

Cooking time: 10 minutes

Servings: 10 people

Ingredients:

- salt and pepper according to taste
- 2 tbsp. of parsley
- 1 vegan pizza dough
- 1 shallot, chopped

- 1 cup of oyster mushrooms, chopped
- ¼ red bell pepper, chopped

Directions:

1. Preheat your air fryer to about 400°F.
2. Cut the pie dough into small squares. Just set them aside.
3. Put your bell pepper, shallot, oyster mushroom, and parsley all together into a mixing dish.
4. According to taste, sprinkle with some pepper and salt.
5. On top of your pizza cubes, put your topping.
6. Put your pizza cubes into your air fryer and cook for about 10 minutes.

2. Veggies Stuffed Eggplants

Preparation time: 5 minutes

Cooking time: 14 minutes

Servings: 5 people

Ingredients:

- 2 tbsp. of tomato paste
- Salt and ground black pepper, as required
- ½ tsp. of garlic, chopped
- 1 tbsp. of vegetable oil
- 1 tbsp. of fresh lime juice
- ½ green bell pepper, seeded and chopped
- ¼ cup of cottage cheese, chopped
- 1 tomato, chopped
- 1 onion, chopped
- 10 small eggplants, halved lengthwise

Directions:

1. Preheat your air fryer to about 320°F and oil the container of your air fryer.
2. Cut a strip longitudinally from all sides of your eggplant and scrape out the pulp in a medium-sized bowl.
3. Add lime juice on top of your eggplants and place them in the container of your Air Fryer.

4. Cook for around a couple of minutes and extract from your Air Fryer.

5. Heat the vegetable oil on medium-high heat in a pan and add the onion and garlic.

6. Sauté for around 2 minutes and mix in the tomato, salt, eggplant flesh, and black pepper.

7. Sauté and add bell pepper, tomato paste, cheese, and cilantro for roughly 3 minutes.

8. Cook for around a minute and put this paste into your eggplants.

9. Shut each eggplant with its lids and adjust the Air Fryer to 360°F.

10. Organize and bake for around 5 minutes in your Air Fryer Basket.

11. Dish out on a serving tray and eat hot.

3. Air-fried Falafel

Preparation time: 10 minutes

Cooking time: 25 minutes

Servings: 6 people

Ingredients:

- Salt and black pepper according to taste
- 1 teaspoon of chili powder
- 2 teaspoon of ground coriander
- 2 teaspoon of ground cumin
- 1 onion, chopped
- 4 garlic cloves, chopped
- Juice of 1 lemon
- 1 cup of fresh parsley, chopped
- ½ cup of chickpea flour

Directions:

1. Add flour, coriander, chickpeas, lemon juice, parsley, onion, garlic, chili, cumin, salt, turmeric, and pepper to a processor and mix until mixed, not too battery; several chunks should be present.
2. Morph the paste into spheres and hand-press them to ensure that they are still around.
3. Spray using some spray oil and place them in a paper-lined air fryer bucket; if necessary, perform in groups.
4. Cook for about 14 minutes at around 360°F, rotating once mid-way through the cooking process.

5. They must be light brown and crispy.

4. Almond Flour Battered Wings

Preparation time: 10 minutes

Cooking time: 25 minutes

Servings: 4 people

Ingredients:

- Salt and pepper according to taste
- 4 tbsp. of minced garlic
- 2 tbsp. of stevia powder
- 16 pieces of vegan chicken wings
- ¾ cup of almond flour
- ¼ cup of butter, melted

Directions:

1. Preheat your air fryer for about 5 minutes.
2. Mix the stevia powder, almond flour, vegan chicken wings, and garlic in a mixing dish. According to taste, sprinkle with some black pepper and salt.
3. Please put it in the bucket of your air fryer and cook at about 400°F for around 25 minutes.

4. Ensure you give your fryer container a shake midway through the cooking process.
5. Put in a serving dish after cooking and add some melted butter on top. Toss it to coat it completely.

5. Spicy Tofu

Preparation time: 5 minutes

Cooking time: 13 minutes

Servings: 3 people

Ingredients:

- Salt and black pepper, according to taste
- 1 tsp. of garlic powder
- 1 tsp. of onion powder
- 1½ tsp. of paprika
- 1½ tbsp. of avocado oil
- 3 tsp. of cornstarch
- 1 (14-ounces) block extra-firm tofu, pressed and cut into ¾-inch cubes

Directions:

1. Preheat your air fryer to about 390°F and oil the container of your air fryer with some spray oil.

2. In a medium-sized bowl, blend the cornstarch, oil, tofu, and spices and mix to cover properly.

3. In the Air Fryer basket, place the tofu bits and cook for around a minute, flipping twice between the cooking times.

4. On a serving dish, spread out the tofu and enjoy it warm.

6. Sautéed Bacon with Spinach

Preparation time: 5 minutes

Cooking time: 9 minutes

Servings: 2 people

Ingredients:

- 1 garlic clove, minced
- 2 tbsp. of olive oil
- 4-ounce of fresh spinach
- 1 onion, chopped
- 3 meatless bacon slices, chopped

Directions:

1. Preheat your air fryer at about 340° F and oil the air fryer's tray with some olive oil or cooking oil spray.

2. In the Air Fryer basket, put garlic and olive oil.

3. Cook and add in the onions and bacon for around 2 minutes.

4. Cook and mix in the spinach for approximately 3 minutes.

5. Cook for 4 more minutes and plate out in a bowl to eat.

7. Garden Fresh Veggie Medley

Preparation time: 5 minutes

Cooking time: 15 minutes

Servings: 4 people

Ingredients:

- 1 tbsp. of balsamic vinegar
- 1 tbsp. of olive oil
- 2 tbsp. of herbs de Provence
- 2 garlic cloves, minced
- 2 small onions, chopped
- 3 tomatoes, chopped

- 1 zucchini, chopped
- 1 eggplant, chopped
- 2 yellow bell peppers seeded and chopped
- Salt and black pepper, according to taste.

Directions:

1. Preheat your air fryer at about 355° F and oil up the air fryer basket.
2. In a medium-sized bowl, add all the ingredients and toss to cover completely.
3. Move to the basket of your Air Fryer and cook for around 15 minutes.
4. After completing the cooking time, let it sit in the air fryer for around 5 minutes and plate out to serve warm.

8. Colorful Vegetable Croquettes

Preparation time: 5 minutes

Cooking time: 10 minutes

Servings: 4 people

Ingredients:

- 1/2 cup of parmesan cheese, grated
- 2 eggs

- 1/4 cup of coconut flour
- 1/2 cup of almond flour
- 2 tbsp. of olive oil
- 3 tbsp. of scallions, minced
- 1 clove garlic, minced
- 1 bell pepper, chopped
- 1/2 cup of mushrooms, chopped
- 1/2 tsp. of cayenne pepper
- Salt and black pepper, according to taste.
- 2 tbsp. of butter
- 4 tbsp. of milk
- 1/2 pound of broccoli

Directions:

1. Boil your broccoli in a medium-sized saucepan for up to around 20 minutes. With butter, milk, black pepper, salt, and cayenne pepper, rinse the broccoli and mash it.

2. Add in the bell pepper, mushrooms, garlic, scallions, and olive oil and blend properly. Form into patties with the blend.

3. Put the flour in a deep bowl; beat your eggs in a second bowl; then put the parmesan cheese in another bowl.

4. Dip each patty into your flour, accompanied by the eggs and lastly the parmesan cheese, push to hold the shape.

5. Cook for around 16 minutes, turning midway through the cooking period, in the preheated Air Fryer at about 370° F. Bon appétit!

9. Cheesy Mushrooms

Preparation time: 3 minutes

Cooking time: 8 minutes

Servings: 4 people

Ingredients:

- 1 tsp. of dried dill
- 2 tbsp. of Italian dried mixed herbs
- 2 tbsp. of olive oil
- 2 tbsp. of cheddar cheese, grated
- 2 tbsp. of mozzarella cheese, grated

- Salt and freshly ground black pepper, according to taste
- 6-ounce of button mushrooms stemmed

Directions:

Preheat the air fryer at around 355° F and oil your air fryer basket.

In a mixing bowl, combine the Italian dried mixed herbs, mushrooms, salt, oil, and black pepper and mix well to cover.

In the Air Fryer bucket, place the mushrooms and cover them with some cheddar cheese and mozzarella cheese.

To eat, cook for around 8 minutes and scatter with dried dill.

10. Greek-style Roasted Vegetables

Preparation time: 10 minutes

Cooking time: 25 minutes

Servings: 3 people

Ingredients:

- 1/2 cup of Kalamata olives, pitted
- 1 (28-ounce) canned diced tomatoes with juice
- 1/2 tsp. of dried basil

- Sea salt and freshly cracked black pepper, according to taste
- 1 tsp. of dried rosemary
- 1 cup of dry white wine
- 2 tbsp. of extra-virgin olive oil
- 2 bell peppers, cut into 1-inch chunks
- 1 red onion, sliced
- 1/2 pound of zucchini, cut into 1-inch chunks
- 1/2 pound of cauliflower, cut into 1-inch florets
- 1/2 pound of butternut squash, peeled and cut into 1-inch chunks

Directions:

1. Add some rosemary, wine, olive oil, black pepper, salt, and basil along with your vegetables toss until well-seasoned.
2. Onto a lightly oiled baking dish, add 1/2 of the canned chopped tomatoes; scatter to fill the base of your baking dish.
3. Add in the vegetables and add the leftover chopped tomatoes to the top. On top of tomatoes, spread the Kalamata olives.

4. Bake for around 20 minutes at about 390° F in the preheated Air Fryer, turning the dish midway through your cooking cycle. Serve it hot and enjoy it!

11. Vegetable Kabobs with Simple Peanut Sauce

Preparation time: 10 minutes

Cooking time: 30 minutes

Servings: 4 people

Ingredients:

- 1/3 tsp. of granulated garlic
- 1 tsp. of dried rosemary, crushed
- 1 tsp. of red pepper flakes, crushed
- Sea salt and ground black pepper, according to your taste.
- 2 tbsp. of extra-virgin olive oil
- 8 small button mushrooms, cleaned
- 8 pearl onions, halved
- 2 bell peppers, diced into 1-inch pieces
- 8 whole baby potatoes, diced into 1-inch pieces

Peanut Sauce:

- 1/2 tsp. of garlic salt

- 1 tbsp. of soy sauce
- 1 tbsp. of balsamic vinegar
- 2 tbsp. of peanut butter

Directions:

1. For a few minutes, dunk the wooden chopsticks in water.

2. String the vegetables onto your chopsticks; drip some olive oil all over your chopsticks with the vegetables on it; dust with seasoning.

3. Cook for about 1 minute at 400°F in the preheated Air Fryer.

Peanut Sauce:

1. In the meantime, mix the balsamic vinegar with some peanut butter, garlic salt and some soy sauce in a tiny dish. Offer the kabobs with a side of peanut sauce. Eat warm!

12. Hungarian Mushroom Pilaf

Preparation time: 10 minutes

Cooking time: 50 minutes

Servings: 4 people

Ingredients:

- 1 tsp. of sweet Hungarian paprika
- 1/2 tsp. of dried tarragon
- 1 tsp. of dried thyme
- 1/4 cup of dry vermouth
- 1 onion, chopped
- 2 garlic cloves
- 2 tbsp. of olive oil
- 1 pound of fresh porcini mushrooms, sliced
- 2 tbsp. of olive oil
- 3 cups of vegetable broth
- 1 ½ cups of white rice

Directions:

1. In a wide saucepan, put the broth and rice, add some water, and bring it to a boil.

2. Cover with a lid and turn the flame down to a low temperature and proceed to cook for the next 18 minutes or so. After cooking, let it rest for 5 to 10 minutes, and then set aside.

3. Finally, in a lightly oiled baking dish, mix the heated, fully cooked rice with the rest of your ingredients.

4. Cook at about 200° degrees for around 20 minutes in the preheated Air Fryer, regularly monitoring to even cook.

5. In small bowls, serve. Bon appétit!

13. Chinese cabbage Bake

Preparation time: 15 minutes

Cooking time: 35 minutes

Servings: 4 people

Ingredients:

- 1 cup of Monterey Jack cheese, shredded
- 1/2 tsp. of cayenne pepper
- 1 cup of cream cheese
- 1/2 cup of milk
- 4 tbsp. of flaxseed meal
- 1/2 stick butter
- 2 garlic cloves, sliced
- 1 onion, thickly sliced
- 1 jalapeno pepper, seeded and sliced

- Sea salt and freshly ground black pepper, according to taste.
- 2 bell peppers, seeded and sliced
- 1/2 pound of Chinese cabbage, roughly chopped

Directions:

1. Heat the salted water in a pan and carry it to a boil. For around 2 to 3 minutes, steam the Chinese cabbage. To end the cooking process, switch the Chinese cabbage to cold water immediately.

2. Put your Chinese cabbage in a lightly oiled casserole dish. Add in the garlic, onion, and peppers.

3. Next, over low fire, melt some butter in a skillet. Add in your flaxseed meal steadily and cook for around 2 minutes to create a paste.

4. Add in the milk gently, constantly whisking until it creates a dense mixture. Add in your cream cheese. Sprinkle some cayenne pepper, salt, and black pepper. To the casserole tray, transfer your mixture.

5. Cover with some Monterey Jack cheese and cook for about 2 minutes at around 390° F in your preheated Air Fryer. Serve it warm.

14. Brussels sprouts With Balsamic Oil

Preparation time: 5 minutes

Cooking time: 15 minutes

Servings: 4 people

Ingredients:

- 2 tbsp. of olive oil
- 2 cups of Brussels sprouts, halved
- 1 tbsp. of balsamic vinegar
- ¼ tsp. of salt

Directions:

1. For 5 minutes, preheat your air fryer.
2. In a mixing bowl, blend all of your ingredients to ensure the zucchini fries are very well coated. Put the fries in the basket of an air fryer.
3. Close it and cook it at about 350°F for around 15 minutes.

15. Aromatic Baked Potatoes with Chives

Preparation time: 15 minutes

Cooking time: 45 minutes

Servings: 2 people

Ingredients:

- 2 tbsp. of chives, chopped
- 2 garlic cloves, minced
- 1 tbsp. of sea salt
- 1/4 tsp. of smoked paprika
- 1/4 tsp. of red pepper flakes
- 2 tbsp. of olive oil
- 4 medium baking potatoes, peeled

Directions:

1. Toss the potatoes with your seasoning, olive oil, and garlic.
2. Please put them in the basket of your Air Fryer. Cook at about 400° F for around 40 minutes just until the potatoes are fork soft in your preheated Air Fryer.
3. Add in some fresh minced chives to garnish. Bon appétit!

16. Easy Vegan "chicken"

Preparation time: 10 minutes

Cooking time: 20 minutes

Servings: 4 people

Ingredients:

- 1 tsp. of celery seeds
- 1/2 tsp. of mustard powder
- 1 tsp. of cayenne pepper
- 1/4 cup of all-purpose flour
- 1/2 cup of cornmeal
- 8 ounces of soy chunks
- Sea salt and ground black pepper, according to taste.

Directions:

1. In a skillet over medium-high flame, cook the soya chunks in plenty of water. Turn off the flame and allow soaking for several minutes. Drain the remaining water, wash, and strain it out.

2. In a mixing bowl, combine the rest of the components. Roll your soy chunks over the breading paste, pressing lightly to stick.

3. In the slightly oiled Air Fryer basket, place your soy chunks.

4. Cook at about 390° for around 10 minutes in your preheated Air Fryer, rotating them over midway

through the cooking process; operate in batches if required. Bon appétit!

17. Paprika Vegetable Kebab's

Preparation time: 10 minutes

Cooking time: 20 minutes

Servings: 4 people

Ingredients:

- 1/2 tsp. of ground black pepper
- 1 tsp. of sea salt flakes
- 1 tsp. of smoked paprika
- 1/4 cup of sesame oil
- 2 tbsp. of dry white wine
- 1 red onion, cut into wedges

- 2 cloves garlic, pressed
- 1 tsp. of whole grain mustard
- 1 fennel bulb, diced
- 1 parsnip, cut into thick slices
- 1 celery, cut into thick slices

Directions:

1. Toss all of the above ingredients together in a mixing bowl to uniformly coat. Thread the vegetables alternately onto the wooden skewers.
2. Cook for around 15 minutes at about 380° F on your Air Fryer grill plate.
3. Turn them over midway during the cooking process.
4. Taste, change the seasonings if needed and serve steaming hot.

18. Spiced Soy Curls

Preparation time: 5 minutes

Cooking time: 10 minutes

Servings: 2 people

Ingredients:

- 1 tsp. of poultry seasoning
- 2 tsp. of Cajun seasoning
- ¼ cup of fine ground cornmeal
- ¼ cup of nutritional yeast
- 4 ounces of soy curls
- 3 cups of boiling water
- Salt and ground white pepper, as needed

Directions:

1. Dip the soy curls for around a minute or so in hot water in a heat-resistant tub.
2. Drain your soy coils using a strainer and force the excess moisture out using a broad spoon.
3. Mix the cornmeal, nutritional yeast, salt, seasonings, and white pepper well in a mixing bowl.
4. Transfer your soy curls to the bowl and coat well with the blend. Let the air-fryer temperature to about 380° F. Oil the basket of your air fryers.
5. Adjust soy curls in a uniform layer in the lined air fryer basket. Cook for about 10 minutes in the air fryer, turning midway through the cycle.

6. Take out the soy curls from your air fryer and put them on a serving dish. Serve it steaming hot.

19. Cauliflower & Egg Rice Casserole

Preparation time: 5 minutes

Cooking time: 15 minutes

Servings: 4 people

Ingredients:

- 2 eggs, beaten
- 1 tablespoon of soy sauce
- Salt and black pepper according to taste.
- ½ cup of chopped onion
- 1 cup of okra, chopped
- 1 yellow bell pepper, chopped
- 2 teaspoon of olive oil

Directions:

1. Preheat your air fryer to about 380° F. Oil a baking tray with spray oil. Pulse the cauliflower till it becomes like thin rice-like capsules in your food blender.

2. Now add your cauliflower rice to a baking tray mix in the okra, bell pepper, salt, soy sauce, onion, and pepper and combine well.

3. Drizzle a little olive oil on top along with the beaten eggs. Put the tray in your air fryer and cook for about a minute. Serve it hot.

20. Hollandaise Topped Grilled Asparagus

Preparation time: 2 minutes

Cooking time: 15 minutes

Servings: 6 people

Ingredients:

- A punch of ground white pepper
- A pinch of mustard powder
- 3 pounds of asparagus spears, trimmed
- 3 egg yolks
- 2 tbsp. of olive oil
- 1 tsp. of chopped tarragon leaves
- ½ tsp. of salt
- ½ lemon juice
- ½ cup of butter, melted

- ¼ tsp. of black pepper

Directions:

1. Preheat your air fryer to about 330° F. In your air fryer, put the grill pan attachment.

2. Mix the olive oil, salt, asparagus, and pepper into a Ziploc bag. To mix all, give everything a quick shake. Load onto the grill plate and cook for about 15 minutes.

3. In the meantime, beat the lemon juice, egg yolks, and salt in a double boiler over a moderate flame until velvety.

4. Add in the melted butter, mustard powder, and some white pepper. Continue whisking till the mixture is creamy and thick. Serve with tarragon leaves as a garnish.

5. Pour the sauce over the asparagus spears and toss to blend.

21. Crispy Asparagus Dipped In Paprika-garlic Spice

Preparation time: 2 minutes

Cooking time: 15 minutes

Servings: 5 people

Ingredients:

- ¼ cup of almond flour
- ½ tsp. of garlic powder
- ½ tsp. of smoked paprika
- 10 medium asparagus, trimmed
- 2 large eggs, beaten
- 2 tbsp. of parsley, chopped
- Salt and pepper according to your taste

Directions:

1. For about 5 minutes, preheat your air fryer.
2. Mix the almond flour, garlic powder, parsley, and smoked paprika in a mixing dish. To taste, season with some salt and black pepper.
3. Soak your asparagus in the beaten eggs, and then dredge it in a combination of almond flour.
4. Put in the bowl of your air fryer. Close the lid. At about 350°F, cook for around a minute.

22. Eggplant Gratin with Mozzarella Crust

Preparation time: 10 minutes

Cooking time: 30 minutes

Servings: 2 people

Ingredients:

- 1 tablespoon of breadcrumbs
- ¼ cup of grated mozzarella cheese
- Cooking spray
- Salt and pepper according to your taste
- ¼ teaspoon of dried marjoram
- ¼ teaspoon of dried basil
- 1 teaspoon of capers
- 1 tablespoon of sliced pimiento-stuffed olives
- 1 clove garlic, minced
- ⅓ cup of chopped tomatoes
- ¼ cup of chopped onion
- ¼ cup of chopped green pepper
- ¼ cup of chopped red pepper

Directions:

1. Put the green pepper, eggplant, onion, red pepper, olives, tomatoes, basil marjoram, garlic, salt, capers, and pepper in a container and preheat your air fryer to about 300° F.

2. Lightly oil a baking tray with a spray of cooking olive oil.

3. Fill your baking with the eggplant combination and line it with the vessel.

4. Place some mozzarella cheese on top of it and top with some breadcrumbs. Put the dish in the frying pan and cook for a few minutes.

23. Asian-style Cauliflower

Preparation time: 10 minutes

Cooking time: 25 minutes

Servings: 4 people

Ingredients:

- 2 tbsp. of sesame seeds
- 1/4 cup of lime juice
- 1 tbsp. of fresh parsley, finely chopped
- 1 tbsp. of ginger, freshly grated
- 2 cloves of garlic, peeled and pressed
- 1 tbsp. of sake
- 1 tbsp. of tamari sauce
- 1 tbsp. of sesame oil

- 1 onion, peeled and finely chopped
- 2 cups of cauliflower, grated

Directions:

1. In a mixing bowl, mix your onion, cauliflower, tamari sauce, sesame oil, garlic, sake, and ginger; whisk until all is well integrated.
2. Air-fry it for around a minute at about 400° F.
3. Pause your Air Fryer. Add in some parsley and lemon juice.
4. Cook for an extra 10 minutes at about 300° degrees F in the air fryer.
5. In the meantime, in a non-stick pan, toast your sesame seeds; swirl them continuously over medium-low heat. Serve hot on top of the cauliflower with a pinch of salt and pepper.

24. Two-cheese Vegetable Frittata

Preparation time: 15 minutes

Cooking time: 35 minutes

Servings: 2 people

Ingredients:

- ⅓ cup of crumbled Feta cheese
- ⅓ cup of grated Cheddar cheese
- Salt and pepper according to taste
- ⅓ cup of milk
- 4 eggs, cracked into a bowl
- 2 teaspoon of olive oil
- ¼ lb. of asparagus, trimmed and sliced thinly
- ¼ cup of chopped chives
- 1 small red onion, sliced
- 1 large zucchini, sliced with a 1-inch thickness
- ⅓ cup of sliced mushrooms

Directions:

1. Preheat your air fryer to about 380° F. Set aside your baking dish lined with some parchment paper. Put salt, milk, and pepper into the egg bowl; whisk evenly.

2. Put a skillet on the stovetop over a moderate flame, and heat your olive oil. Add in the zucchini, asparagus, baby spinach, onion, and mushrooms; stir-fry for around 5 minutes. Transfer the vegetables into your baking tray, and finish with the beaten egg.

3. Put the tray into your air fryer and finish with cheddar and feta cheese.

4. For about 15 minutes, cook. Take out your baking tray and add in some fresh chives to garnish.

25. Rice & Beans Stuffed Bell Peppers

Preparation time: 10 minutes

Cooking time: 15 minutes

Servings: 5 people

Ingredients:

- 1 tbsp. of Parmesan cheese, grated
- ½ cup of mozzarella cheese, shredded
- 5 large bell peppers, tops removed and seeded
- 1½ tsp. of Italian seasoning
- 1 cup of cooked rice
- 1 (15-ounces) can of red kidney beans, rinsed and drained
- 1 (15-ounces) can of diced tomatoes with juice
- ½ small bell pepper, seeded and chopped

Directions:

1. Combine the tomatoes with juice, bell pepper, rice, beans, and Italian seasoning in a mixing dish. Using the rice mixture, fill each bell pepper uniformly.

2. Preheat the air fryer to 300° F. Oil the basket of your air fryer with some spray oil. Put the bell peppers in a uniform layer in your air fryer basket.

3. Cook for around 12 minutes in the air fryer. In the meantime, combine the Parmesan and mozzarella cheese in a mixing dish.

4. Remove the peppers from the air fryer basket and top each with some cheese mix. Cook for another 3 -4 minutes in the air fryer

5. Take the bell peppers from the air fryer and put them on a serving dish. Enable to cool slowly before serving. Serve it hot.

26. Parsley-loaded Mushrooms

Preparation time: 5 minutes

Cooking time: 15 minutes

Servings: 2 people

Ingredients:

- 2 tablespoon of parsley, finely chopped
- 2 teaspoon of olive oil
- 1 garlic clove, crushed
- 2 slices white bread
- salt and black pepper according to your taste

Directions:

1. Preheat the air fryer to about 360° F. Crush your bread into crumbs in a food blender. Add the parsley, garlic, and pepper; blend with the olive oil and mix.

2. Remove the stalks from the mushrooms and stuff the caps with breadcrumbs. In your air fryer basket, position the mushroom heads. Cook for a few minutes, just until golden brown and crispy.

27. Cheesy Vegetable Quesadilla

Preparation time: 2 minutes

Cooking time: 15 minutes

Servings: 1 people

Ingredients:

- 1 teaspoon of olive oil

- 1 tablespoon of cilantro, chopped
- ½ green onion, sliced
- ¼ zucchini, sliced
- ¼ yellow bell pepper, sliced
- ¼ cup of shredded gouda cheese

Directions:

1. Preheat your air fryer to about 390° F. Oil a basket of air fryers with some cooking oil.

2. Put a flour tortilla in your air fryer basket and cover it with some bell pepper, Gouda cheese, cilantro, zucchini, and green onion. Take the other tortilla to cover and spray with some olive oil.

3. Cook until slightly golden brown, for around 10 minutes. Cut into 4 slices for serving when ready. Enjoy!

28. Creamy 'n Cheese Broccoli Bake

Preparation time: 10 minutes

Cooking time: 30 minutes

Servings: 2 people

Ingredients:

- 1/4 cup of water
- 1-1/2 teaspoons of butter, or to taste
- 1/2 cup of cubed sharp Cheddar cheese
- 1/2 (14 ounces) can evaporate milk, divided
- 1/2 large onion, coarsely diced
- 1 tbsp. of dry bread crumbs, or to taste
- salt according to taste
- 2 tbsp. of all-purpose flour
- 1-pound of fresh broccoli, coarsely diced

Directions:

1. Lightly oil the air-fryer baking pan with cooking oil. Add half of the milk and flour into a pan and simmer at about 360° F for around 5 minutes.

2. Mix well midway through the cooking period. Remove the broccoli and the extra milk. Cook for the next 5 minutes after fully blending.

3. Mix in the cheese until it is fully melted. Mix the butter and bread crumbs well in a shallow tub. Sprinkle the broccoli on top.

4. At about 360° F, cook for around 20 minutes until the tops are finely golden brown. Enjoy and serve warm.

29. Sweet & Spicy Parsnips

Preparation time: 12 minutes

Cooking time: 44 minutes

Servings: 6 people

Ingredients:

- ¼ tsp. of red pepper flakes, crushed
- 1 tbsp. of dried parsley flakes, crushed
- 2 tbsp. of honey
- 1 tbsp. of n butter, melted
- 2 pounds of a parsnip, peeled and cut into 1-inch chunks
- Salt and ground black pepper, according to your taste.

Directions:

1. Let the air-fryer temperature to about 355° F. Oil the basket of your air fryers. Combine the butter and parsnips in a big dish.
2. Transfer the parsnip pieces into the lined air fryer basket arranges them in a uniform layer. Cook for a few minutes in the fryer.

3. In the meantime, combine the leftover ingredients in a large mixing bowl.

4. Move the parsnips into the honey mixture bowl after around 40 minutes and toss them to coat properly.

5. Again, in a uniform layer, organize the parsnip chunks into your air fryer basket.

6. Air-fry for another 3-4 minutes. Take the parsnip pieces from the air fryer and pass them onto the serving dish. Serve it warm.

30. Zucchini with Mediterranean Dill Sauce

Preparation time: 20 minutes

Cooking time: 60 minutes

Servings: 4 people

Ingredients:

- 1/2 tsp. of freshly cracked black peppercorns
- 2 sprigs thyme, leaves only, crushed
- 1 sprig rosemary, leaves only, crushed
- 1 tsp. of sea salt flakes
- 2 tbsp. of melted butter
- 1 pound of zucchini, peeled and cubed

For your Mediterranean Dipping:

- 1 tbsp. of olive oil

- 1 tbsp. of fresh dill, chopped

- 1/3 cup of yogurt

- 1/2 cup of mascarpone cheese

Directions:

1. To start, preheat your Air Fryer to 350° F. Now, add ice cold water to the container with your potato cubes and let them sit in the bath for about 35 minutes.

2. Dry your potato cubes with a hand towel after that. Whisk together the sea salt flakes, melted butter, thyme, rosemary, and freshly crushed peppercorns in a mixing container. This butter/spice mixture can be rubbed onto the potato cubes.

3. In the cooking basket of your air fryer, air-fry your potato cubes for around 18 to 20 minutes or until cooked completely; ensure you shake the potatoes at least once during cooking to cook them uniformly.

4. In the meantime, by mixing the rest of the ingredients, create the Mediterranean dipping sauce. To dip and eat, serve warm potatoes with Mediterranean sauce!

31. Zesty Broccoli

Preparation time: 10 minutes

Cooking time: 15 minutes

Servings: 4 people

Ingredients:

- 1 tbsp. of butter
- 1 large crown broccoli, chopped into bite-sized pieces
- 1 tbsp. of white sesame seeds
- 2 tbsp. of vegetable stock
- ½ tsp. of red pepper flakes, crushed
- 3 garlic cloves, minced
- ½ tsp. of fresh lemon zest, grated finely
- 1 tbsp. of pure lemon juice

Directions:

1. Preheat the Air fryer to about 355° F and oil an Air fryer pan with cooking spray. In the Air fryer plate, combine the vegetable stock, butter, and lemon juice.

2. Move the mixture and cook for about 2 minutes into your Air Fryer. Cook for a minute after incorporating the broccoli and garlic.

3. Cook for a minute with lemon zest, sesame seeds, and red pepper flakes. Remove the dish from the oven and eat immediately.

32. Chewy Glazed Parsnips

Preparation time: 15 minutes

Cooking time: 44 minutes

Servings: 6 people

Ingredients:

- ¼ tsp. of red pepper flakes, crushed
- 1 tbsp. of dried parsley flakes, crushed
- 2 tbsp. of maple syrup
- 1 tbsp. of butter, melted
- 2 pounds of parsnips, skinned and chopped into 1-inch chunks

Directions:

1. Preheat the Air fryer to about 355° F and oil your air fryer basket. In a wide mixing bowl, combine the butter and parsnips and toss well to cover. Cook for around 40 minutes with the parsnips in the Air fryer basket.

2. In the meantime, combine in a wide bowl the rest of your ingredients. Move this mix to your basket of the air fryer and cook for another 4 minutes or so. Remove the dish from the oven and eat promptly.

33. Hoisin-glazed Bok Choy

Preparation time: 5 minutes

Cooking time: 10 minutes

Servings: 4 people

Ingredients:

- 1 tbsp. of all-purpose flour
- 2 tbsp. of sesame oil
- 2 tbsp. of hoisin sauce
- 1/2 tsp. of sage
- 1 tsp. of onion powder
- 2 garlic cloves, minced
- 1 pound of baby Bok choy, roots removed, leaves separated

Directions:

1. In a lightly oiled Air Fryer basket, put the onion powder, garlic, Bok Choy, and sage. Cook for around 3 minutes at about 350° F in a preheated Air Fryer.

2. Whisk together the sesame oil, hoisin sauce, and flour in a deep mixing dish. Drizzle over the Bok choy with the gravy. Cook for an extra minute. Bon appétit!

34. Green Beans with Okra

Preparation time: 10 minutes

Cooking time: 20 minutes

Servings: 2 people

Ingredients:

- 3 tbsp. of balsamic vinegar
- ¼ cup of nutritional yeast
- ½ (10-ounces) of bag chilled cut green beans
- ½ (10-ounces) of bag chilled cut okra
- Salt and black pepper, according to your taste.

Directions:

1. Preheat your Air fryer to about 400° F and oil the air fryer basket.

2. In a wide mixing bowl, toss together the salt, green beans, okra, vinegar, nutritional yeast, and black pepper.

3. Cook for around 20 minutes with the okra mixture in your Air fryer basket. Dish out into a serving plate and eat warm.

35. Celeriac with some Greek Yogurt Dip

Preparation time: 12 minutes

Cooking time: 25 minutes

Servings: 2 people

Ingredients:

- 1/2 tsp. of sea salt
- 1/2 tsp. of ground black pepper, to taste
- 1 tbsp. of sesame oil
- 1 red onion, chopped into 1 1/2-inch piece
- 1/2 pound of celeriac, chopped into 1 1/2-inch piece

Spiced Yogurt:

- 1/2 tsp. of chili powder
- 1/2 tsp. of mustard seeds
- 2 tbsp. of mayonnaise

- 1/4 cup of Greek yogurt

Directions:

1. In the slightly oiled cooking basket, put the veggies in one uniform layer. Pour sesame oil over the veggies.
2. Season with a pinch of black pepper and a pinch of salt. Cook for around 20 minutes at about 300° F, tossing the basket midway through your cooking cycle.
3. In the meantime, whisk all the leftover ingredients into the sauce. Spoon the sauce over the veggies that have been cooked. Bon appétit!

36. Wine & Garlic Flavored Vegetables

Preparation time: 7-10 minutes

Cooking time: 15 minutes

Servings: 4 people

Ingredients:

- 4 cloves of garlic, minced
- 3 tbsp. of red wine vinegar
- 1/3 cup of olive oil
- 1 red onion, diced

- 1 package frozen diced vegetables
- 1 cup of baby Portobello mushrooms, diced
- 1 tsp. of Dijon mustard
- 1 ½ tbsp. of honey
- Salt and pepper according to your taste
- ¼ cup of chopped fresh basil

Directions:

1. Preheat the air fryer to about 330° F. In the air fryer, put the grill pan attachment.

2. Combine the veggies and season with pepper, salt, and garlic in a Ziploc container. To mix all, give everything a strong shake. Dump and cook for around 15 minutes on the grill pan.

3. Additionally, add the remainder of the ingredients into a mixing bowl and season with some more salt and pepper. Drizzle the sauce over your grilled vegetables.

37. Spicy Braised Vegetables

Preparation time: 10 minutes

Cooking time: 25 minutes

Servings: 4 people

Ingredients:

- 1/2 cup of tomato puree
- 1/4 tsp. of ground black pepper
- 1/2 tsp. of fine sea salt
- 1 tbsp. of garlic powder
- 1/2 tsp. of fennel seeds
- 1/4 tsp. of mustard powder
- 1/2 tsp. of porcini powder
- 1/4 cup of olive oil
- 1 celery stalk, chopped into matchsticks
- 2 bell peppers, deveined and thinly diced
- 1 Serrano pepper, deveined and thinly diced
- 1 large-sized zucchini, diced

Directions:

1. In your Air Fryer cooking basket, put your peppers, zucchini, sweet potatoes, and carrot.
2. Drizzle with some olive oil and toss to cover completely; cook for around 15 minutes in a preheated Air Fryer at about 350°F.

3. Make the sauce as the vegetables are frying by quickly whisking the remaining ingredients (except the tomato ketchup). Slightly oil up a baking dish that fits your fryer.

4. Add the cooked vegetables to the baking dish, along with the sauce, and toss well to cover.

5. Turn the Air Fryer to about 390° F and cook for 2-4 more minutes with the vegetables. Bon appétit!

CHAPTER 3: Air Fryer Snack Side Dishes and Appetizer Recipes

1. Crispy 'n Tasty Spring Rolls

Preparation time: 5 minutes

Cooking time: 15 minutes

Servings: 4 people

Ingredients:

- 8 spring roll wrappers
- 1 tsp. of nutritional yeast
- 1 tsp. of corn starch + 2 tablespoon water
- 1 tsp. of coconut sugar
- 1 tbsp. of soy sauce
- 1 medium carrot, shredded
- 1 cup of shiitake mushroom, sliced thinly
- 1 celery stalk, chopped
- ½ tsp. of ginger, finely chopped

Directions:

1. Mix your carrots, celery stalk, soy sauce, coconut sugar, ginger, and nutritional yeast with each other in a mixing dish.

2. Have a tbsp. of your vegetable mix and put it in the middle of your spring roll wrappers.

3. Roll up and secure the sides of your wraps with some cornstarch.

4. Cook for about 15 minutes or till your spring roll wraps is crisp in a preheated air fryer at 200F.

2. Spinach & Feta Crescent Triangles

Preparation time: 10 minutes

Cooking time: 20 minutes

Servings: 4 people

Ingredients:

- ¼ teaspoon of salt
- 1 teaspoon of chopped oregano
- ¼ teaspoon of garlic powder
- 1 cup of crumbled feta cheese

- 1 cup of steamed spinach

Directions:

1. Preheat your air fryer to about 350 F, and then roll up the dough over a level surface that is gently floured.

2. In a medium-sized bowl, mix the spinach, feta, salt, oregano, and ground garlic cloves. Split your dough into four equal chunks.

3. Split the mix of feta/spinach among the four chunks of dough. Fold and seal your dough using a fork.

4. Please put it on a baking tray covered with parchment paper, and then put it in your air fryer.

5. Cook until nicely golden, for around 1 minute.

3. Healthy Avocado Fries

Preparation time: 5 minutes

Cooking time: 20 minutes

Servings: 2 people

Ingredients:

- ¼ cup of aquafaba
- 1 avocado, cubed
- Salt as required

Directions:

1. Mix the aquafaba, crumbs, and salt in a mixing bowl.

2. Preheat your air fryer to about 390°F and cover the avocado pieces uniformly in the crumbs blend.

3. Put the ready pieces in the cooking bucket of your air fryer and cook for several minutes.

4. Twice-fried Cauliflower Tater Tots

Preparation time: 5 minutes

Cooking time: 16 minutes

Servings: 12 people

Ingredients:

- 3 tbsp. Of oats flaxseed meal + 3 tbsp. of water)
- 1-pound of cauliflower, steamed and chopped
- 1 tsp. of parsley, chopped
- 1 tsp. of oregano, chopped
- 1 tsp. of garlic, minced
- 1 tsp. of chives, chopped
- 1 onion, chopped
- 1 flax egg (1 tablespoon 3 tablespoon desiccated coconuts)

- ½ cup of nutritional yeast
- salt and pepper according to taste
- ½ cup of bread crumbs

Directions:

1. Preheat your air fryer to about 390 degrees F.
2. To extract extra moisture, place the steamed cauliflower onto a ring and a paper towel.
3. Put and mix the remainder of your ingredients, excluding your bread crumbs, in a small mixing container.
4. Use your palms, blend it until well mixed and shapes into a small ball.
5. Roll your tater tots over your bread crumbs and put them in the bucket of your air fryer.
6. For a minute, bake. Raise the cooking level to about 400 F and cook for the next 10 minutes.

5. Cheesy Mushroom & Cauliflower Balls

Preparation time: 10 minutes

Cooking time: 50 minutes

Servings: 4 people

Ingredients:

- Salt and pepper according to taste
- 2 sprigs chopped fresh thyme
- ¼ cup of coconut oil
- 1 cup of Grana Padano cheese
- 1 cup of breadcrumbs
- 2 tablespoon of vegetable stock
- 3 cups of cauliflower, chopped
- 3 cloves garlic, minced
- 1 small red onion, chopped
- 3 tablespoon of olive oil

Directions:

1. Over moderate flame, put a pan. Add some balsamic vinegar. When the oil is heated, stir-fry your onion and garlic till they become transparent.
2. Add in the mushrooms and cauliflower and stir-fry for about 5 minutes. Add in your stock, add thyme and cook till your cauliflower has consumed the stock. Add pepper, Grana Padano cheese, and salt.

3. Let the mix cool down and form bite-size spheres of your paste. To harden, put it in the fridge for about 30 minutes.

4. Preheat your air fryer to about 350°F.

5. Add your coconut oil and breadcrumbs into a small bowl and blend properly.

6. Take out your mushroom balls from the fridge, swirl the breadcrumb paste once more, and drop the balls into your breadcrumb paste.

7. Avoid overcrowding, put your balls into your air fryer's container and cook for about 15 minutes, flipping after every 5 minutes to ensure even cooking.

8. Serve with some tomato sauce and brown sugar.

6. Italian Seasoned Easy Pasta Chips

Preparation time: 5 minutes

Cooking time: 10 minutes

Servings: 2 people

Ingredients:

- 2 cups of whole wheat bowtie pasta
- 1 tbsp. of olive oil

- 1 tbsp. of nutritional yeast
- 1 ½ tsp. of Italian seasoning blend
- ½ tsp. of salt

Directions:

1. Put the accessory for the baking tray into your air fryer.
2. Mix all the ingredients in a medium-sized bowl, offer it a gentle stir.
3. Add the mixture to your air fryer basket.
4. Close your air fryer and cook at around 400°degrees F for about 10 minutes.

7. Thai Sweet Potato Balls

Preparation time: 10 minutes

Cooking time: 50 minutes

Servings: 4 people

Ingredients:

- 1 cup of coconut flakes
- 1 tsp. of baking powder
- 1/2 cup of almond meal
- 1/4 tsp. of ground cloves

- 1/2 tsp. of ground cinnamon
- 2 tsp. of orange zest
- 1 tbsp. of orange juice
- 1 cup of brown sugar
- 1 pound of sweet potatoes

Directions:

1. Bake your sweet potatoes for around 25 to 30 minutes at about 380° F till they become soft; peel and mash them in a medium-sized bowl.

2. Add orange zest, orange juice, brown sugar, ground cinnamon, almond meal, cloves, and baking powder. Now blend completely.

3. Roll the balls around in some coconut flakes.

4. Bake for around 15 minutes or until fully fried and crunchy in the preheated Air Fryer at about 360° F.

5. For the rest of the ingredients, redo the same procedure. Bon appétit!

8. Barbecue Roasted Almonds

Preparation time: 5 minutes

Cooking time: 20 minutes

Servings: 6 people

Ingredients:

- 1 tbsp. of olive oil
- 1/4 tsp. of smoked paprika
- 1/2 tsp. of cumin powder
- 1/4 tsp. of mustard powder
- 1/4 tsp. of garlic powder
- Sea salt and ground black pepper, according to taste
- 1 ½ cups of raw almonds

Directions:

1. In a mixing pot, mix all your ingredients.
2. Line the container of your Air Fryer with some baking parchment paper. Arrange the covered almonds out in the basket of your air fryer in a uniform layer.
3. Roast for around 8 to 9 minutes at about 340°F, tossing the bucket once or twice. If required, work in groups.
4. Enjoy!

9. Croissant Rolls

Preparation time: 2 minutes

Cooking time: 6 minutes

Servings: 8 people

Ingredients:

- 4 tbsp. of butter, melted
- 1 (8-ounces) can croissant rolls

Directions:

1. Adjust the air-fryer temperature to about 320°F. Oil the basket of your air fryers.
2. Into your air fryer basket, place your prepared croissant rolls.
3. Airs fry them for around 4 minutes or so.
4. Flip to the opposite side and cook for another 2-3 minutes.
5. Take out from your air fryer and move to a tray.
6. Glaze with some melted butter and eat warm.

10. Curry' n Coriander Spiced Bread Rolls

Preparation time: 5 minutes

Cooking time: 15 minutes

Servings: 5 people

Ingredients:

- salt and pepper according to taste
- 5 large potatoes, boiled
- 2 sprigs, curry leaves
- 2 small onions, chopped
- 2 green chilies, seeded and chopped
- 1 tbsp. of olive oil
- 1 bunch of coriander, chopped
- ½ tsp. of turmeric
- 8 slices of vegan wheat bread, brown sides discarded
- ½ tsp. of mustard seeds

Directions:

1. Mash your potatoes in a bowl and sprinkle some black pepper and salt according to taste. Now set aside.

2. In a pan, warm up the olive oil over medium-low heat and add some mustard seeds. Mix until the seeds start to sputter.

3. Now add in the onions and cook till they become transparent. Mix in the curry leaves and turmeric powder.

4. Keep on cooking till it becomes fragrant for a couple of minutes. Take it off the flame and add the mixture to the potatoes.

5. Mix in the green chilies and some coriander. This is meant to be the filling.

6. Wet your bread and drain excess moisture. In the center of the loaf, put a tbsp. of the potato filling and gently roll the bread so that the potato filling is fully enclosed within the bread.

7. Brush with some oil and put them inside your air fryer basket.

8. Cook for around 15 minutes in a preheated air fryer at about 400°F.

9. Ensure that the air fryer basket is shaken softly midway through the cooking period for an even cooking cycle.

11. Scrumptiously Healthy Chips

Preparation time: 5 minutes

Cooking time: 10 minutes

Servings: 2 people

Ingredients:

- 2 tbsp. of olive oil

- 2 tbsp. of almond flour
- 1 tsp. of garlic powder
- 1 bunch kale
- Salt and pepper according to taste

Directions:

1. For around 5 minutes, preheat your air fryer.
2. In a mixing bowl, add all your ingredients, add the kale leaves at the end and toss to completely cover them.
3. Put in the basket of your fryer and cook until crispy for around 10 minutes.

12. Kid-friendly Vegetable Fritters

Preparation time: 5 minutes

Cooking time: 20 minutes

Servings: 4 people

Ingredients:

- 2 tbsp. of olive oil
- 1/2 cup of cornmeal
- 1/2 cup of all-purpose flour
- 1/2 tsp. of ground cumin

- 1 tsp. of turmeric powder
- 2 garlic cloves, pressed
- 1 carrot, grated
- 1 sweet pepper, seeded and chopped
- 1 yellow onion, finely chopped
- 1 tbsp. of ground flaxseeds
- Salt and ground black pepper, according to taste
- 1 pound of broccoli florets

Directions:

1. In salted boiling water, blanch your broccoli until al dente, for around 3 to 5 minutes. Drain the excess water and move to a mixing bowl; add in the rest of your ingredients to mash the broccoli florets.

2. Shape the paste into patties and position them in the slightly oiled Air Fryer basket.

3. Cook for around 6 minutes at about 400° F, flipping them over midway through the cooking process; if needed, operate in batches.

4. Serve hot with some Vegenaise of your choice. Enjoy it!

13. Avocado Fries

Preparation time: 10 minutes

Cooking time: 50 minutes

Servings: 4 people

Ingredients:

- 2 avocados, cut into wedges
- 1/2 cup of parmesan cheese, grated
- 2 eggs
- Sea salt and ground black pepper, according to taste.
- 1/2 cup of almond meal
- 1/2 head garlic (6-7 cloves)

Sauce:

- 1 tsp. of mustard
- 1 tsp. of lemon juice
- 1/2 cup of mayonnaise

Directions:

1. On a piece of aluminum foil, put your garlic cloves and spray some cooking spray on it. Wrap your garlic cloves in the foil.

2. Cook for around 1-2 minutes at about 400°F in your preheated Air Fryer. Inspect the garlic, open the foil's top end, and keep cooking for an additional 10-12 minutes.

3. Once done, let them cool for around 10 to 15 minutes; take out the cloves by pressing them out of their skin; mash your garlic and put them aside.

4. Mix the salt, almond meal, and black pepper in a small dish.

5. Beat the eggs until foamy in a separate bowl.

6. Put some parmesan cheese in the final shallow dish.

7. In your almond meal blend, dip the avocado wedges, dusting off any excess.

8. In the beaten egg, dunk your wedges; eventually, dip in some parmesan cheese.

9. Spray your avocado wedges on both sides with some cooking oil spray.

10. Cook for around 8 minutes in the preheated Air Fryer at about 395° F, flipping them over midway thru the cooking process.

11. In the meantime, mix the ingredients of your sauce with your cooked crushed garlic.

12. Split the avocado wedges between plates and cover with the sauce before serving. Enjoy!

14. Crispy Wings with Lemony Old Bay Spice

Preparation time: 10 minutes

Cooking time: 25 minutes

Servings: 4 people

Ingredients:

- Salt and pepper according to taste
- 3 pounds of vegan chicken wings
- 1 tsp. of lemon juice, freshly squeezed
- 1 tbsp. of old bay spices
- ¾ cup of almond flour
- ½ cup of butter

Directions:

1. For about 5 minutes, preheat your air fryer. Mix all your ingredients in a mixing dish, excluding the butter. Put in the bowl of an air fryer.

2. Preheat the oven to about 350°F and bake for around 25 minutes. Rock the fryer container midway thru the cooking process, also for cooking.

3. Drizzle with some melted butter when it's done frying. Enjoy!

15. Cold Salad with Veggies and Pasta

Preparation time: 30 minutes

Cooking time: 1 hour 35 minutes

Servings: 12 people

Ingredients:

- ½ cup of fat-free Italian dressing
- 2 tablespoons of olive oil, divided

- ½ cup of Parmesan cheese, grated
- 8 cups of cooked pasta
- 4 medium tomatoes, cut in eighths
- 3 small eggplants, sliced into ½-inch thick rounds
- 3 medium zucchinis, sliced into ½-inch thick rounds
- Salt, according to your taste.

Directions:

1. Preheat your Air fryer to about 355° F and oil the inside of your air fryer basket. In a dish, mix 1 tablespoon of olive oil and zucchini and swirl to cover properly.

2. Cook for around 25 minutes your zucchini pieces in your Air fryer basket. In another dish, mix your eggplants with a tablespoon of olive oil and toss to coat properly.

3. Cook for around 40 minutes your eggplant slices in your Air fryer basket. Re-set the Air Fryer temperature to about 320° F and put the tomatoes next in the ready basket.

4. Cook and mix all your air-fried vegetables for around 30 minutes. To serve, mix in the rest of the ingredients and chill for at least 2 hours, covered.

16. Zucchini and Minty Eggplant Bites

Preparation time: 15 minutes

Cooking time: 35 minutes

Servings: 8 people

Ingredients:

- 3 tbsp. of olive oil
- 1 pound of zucchini, peeled and cubed
- 1 pound of eggplant, peeled and cubed
- 2 tbsp. of melted butter
- 1 ½ tsp. of red pepper chili flakes
- 2 tsp. of fresh mint leaves, minced

Directions:

1. In a large mixing container, add all of the ingredients mentioned above.
2. Roast the zucchini bites and eggplant in your Air Fryer for around 30 minutes at about 300° F, flipping once or twice during the cooking cycle. Serve with some dipping sauce that's homemade.

17. Stuffed Potatoes

Preparation time: 15 minutes

Cooking time: 31 minutes

Servings: 4 people

Ingredients:

- 3 tbsp. of canola oil
- ½ cup of Parmesan cheese, grated
- 2 tbsp. of chives, chopped
- ½ of brown onion, chopped
- 1 tbsp. of butter
- 4 potatoes, peeled

Directions:

1. Preheat the Air fryer to about 390° F and oil the air fryer basket. Coat the canola oil on the potatoes and place them in your Air Fryer Basket.

2. Cook for around 20 minutes before serving on a platter. Halve each potato and scrape out the middle from each half of it.

3. In a frying pan, melt some butter over medium heat and add the onions. Sauté in a bowl for around 5 minutes and dish out.

4. Combine the onions with the middle of the potato, chives and half of the cheese. Stir well and uniformly cram the onion potato mixture into the potato halves.

5. Top and layer the potato halves in your Air Fryer basket with the leftover cheese. Cook for around 6 minutes before serving hot.

18. Paneer Cutlet

Preparation time: 5 minutes

Cooking time: 15 minutes

Servings: 1 people

Ingredients:

- ½ teaspoon of salt
- ½ teaspoon of oregano
- 1 small onion, finely chopped
- ½ teaspoon of garlic powder
- 1 teaspoon of butter
- ½ teaspoon of chai masala

- 1 cup of grated cheese

Directions:

1. Preheat the air fryer to about 350° F and lightly oil a baking dish. In a mixing bowl, add all ingredients and stir well. Split the mixture into cutlets and put them in an oiled baking dish.

2. Put the baking dish in your air fryer and cook your cutlets until crispy, around a minute or so.

19. Spicy Roasted Cashew Nuts

Preparation time: 10 Minutes

Cooking time: 20 Minutes

Servings: 4

Ingredients:

- 1/2 tsp. of ancho chili powder
- 1/2 tsp. of smoked paprika
- Salt and ground black pepper, according to taste
- 1 tsp. of olive oil
- 1 cup of whole cashews

Directions:

1. In a mixing big bowl, toss all your ingredients.

2. Line parchment paper to cover the Air Fryer container. Space out the spiced cashews in your basket in a uniform layer.

3. Roast for about 6 to 8 minutes at 300 degrees F, tossing the basket once or twice during the cooking process. Work in batches if needed. Enjoy!

CHAPTER 4: Deserts

1. Almond-apple Treat

Preparation time: 5 minutes

Cooking time: 15 minutes

Servings: 4 people

Ingredients:

- 2 tablespoon of sugar
- ¾ oz. of raisins
- 1 ½ oz. of almonds

Directions:

1. Preheat your air fryer to around 360° F.
2. Mix the almonds, sugar, and raisins in a dish. Blend using a hand mixer.
3. Load the apples with a combination of the almond mixture. Please put them in the air fryer basket and cook for a few minutes. Enjoy!

2. Pepper-pineapple With Butter-sugar Glaze

Preparation time: 5 minutes

Cooking time: 10 minutes

Servings: 2 people

Ingredients:

- Salt according to taste.
- 2 tsp. of melted butter
- 1 tsp. of brown sugar
- 1 red bell pepper, seeded and julienned
- 1 medium-sized pineapple, peeled and sliced

Directions:

1. To about 390°F, preheat your air fryer. In your air fryer, put the grill pan attachment.
2. In a Ziploc bag, combine all ingredients and shake well.
3. Dump and cook on the grill pan for around 10 minutes to ensure you turn the pineapples over every 5 minutes during cooking.

3. True Churros with Yummy Hot Chocolate

Preparation time: 10 minutes

Cooking time: 25 minutes

Servings: 3 people

Ingredients:

- 1 tsp. of ground cinnamon

- 1/3 cup of sugar
- 1 tbsp. of cornstarch
- 1 cup of milk
- 2 ounces of dark chocolate
- 1 cup of all-purpose flour
- 1 tbsp. of canola oil
- 1 tsp. of lemon zest
- 1/4 tsp. of sea salt
- 2 tbsp. of granulated sugar
- 1/2 cup of water

Directions:

1. To create the churro dough, boil the water in a pan over a medium-high flame; then, add the salt, sugar, and lemon zest and fry, stirring continuously, until fully dissolved.

2. Take the pan off the heat and add in some canola oil. Stir the flour in steadily, constantly stirring until the solution turns to a ball.

3. With a broad star tip, pipe the paste into a piping bag. In the oiled Air Fryer basket, squeeze 4-inch slices of

dough. Cook for around 6 minutes at a temperature of 300° F.

4. Make the hot cocoa for dipping in the meantime. In a shallow saucepan, melt some chocolate and 1/2 cup of milk over low flame.

5. In the leftover 1/2 cup of milk, mix the cornstarch and blend it into the hot chocolate mixture. Cook for around 5 minutes on low flame.

6. Mix the sugar and cinnamon; roll your churros in this combination. Serve with a side of hot cocoa. Enjoy!

Conclusion

These times, air frying is one of the most common cooking techniques and air fryers have become one of the chef's most impressive devices. In no time, air fryers can help you prepare nutritious and tasty meals! To prepare unique dishes for you and your family members, you do not need to be a master in the kitchen.

Everything you have to do is buy an air fryer and this wonderful cookbook for air fryers! Soon, you can make the greatest dishes ever and inspire those around you.

Cooked meals at home with you! Believe us! Get your hands on an air fryer and this handy set of recipes for air fryers and begin your new cooking experience. Have fun!

CPSIA information can be obtained
at www.ICGtesting.com
Printed in the USA
BVHW041012150321
602551BV00006B/424

9 781801 842495